OVERLORD

OVERLORD

═══ POEMS ═══

Jorie Graham

HarperCollins books may be purchased for educational, business, or sales promotional use. For information, please e-mail the Special Markets Department at SPsales@harpercollins.com.

FIRST ECCO PAPERBACK EDITION 2006.

Book Design by Fearn Cutler de Vicq

The Library of Congress has catalogued the hardcover edition as follows:

Graham, Jorie.

Overlord : poems / Jorie Graham.—1st ed.

p. cm.

ISBN 0-06-074565-7

I. Title

PS3557.R214094 2005

811'.54—dc22

2004053681

ISBN-10: 0-06-75811-2 (pbk.) ISBN-13: 978-0-06-075811-0 (pbk.)

18 19 20 21 ❖/RRD 10 9 8 7 6 5 4 3

This book is dedicated to the life of my parents,

Bill and Beverly,

and to the life of my daughter,

Emily.

My gratitude to my brother, John.

For assistance in research, thanks to Susan Barba, Colonel Worman, Jean Pierre and Veronique Onufryk, Isabelle and Yves Michel Payot, and most of all to Hervé Lerendu.

Special thanks to Doug Powell, Brighde Mullins, Peter Richards, Jane Miller, Frank Bidart, Forrest Gander, Fanny Howe, and especially to my editor, Dan Halpern, for his suggestions.

To Peter, love.

Acknowledgment to the editors of *The New Yorker*, the *New York Times*/Op-Ed page, *American Poetry Review*, *Volt*, *New American Writing*, and *Boston Review*, in which these poems first appeared.

CONTENTS

OTHER   1

DAWN DAY ONE   4

PRAYING *(Attempt of June 8 '03)*   8

SOLDATENFRIEDHOF   12

PRAYING *(Attempt of June 6 '03)*   16

UPON EMERGENCE   20

LITTLE EXERCISE   23

PRAYING *(Attempt of May 9 '03)*   24

OMAHA   28

PRAYING *(Attempt of June 14 '03)*   31

SPOKEN FROM THE HEDGEROWS   34

SPOKEN FROM THE HEDGEROWS   37

SPOKEN FROM THE HEDGEROWS   40

DISENCHANTMENT   43

EUROPE *(Omaha Beach 2003)*   50

IMPRESSIONISM   53

PHYSICIAN   58

DISENCHANTMENT   61

PRAYING *(Attempt of Feb 6 '04)* 65

PASSENGER 69

COMMUTE SENTENCE 72

COPY 74

PRAYING *(Attempt of April 19 '04)* 80

COMMUNION 83

POSTERITY 86

NOTES 89

Belief is like a guillotine, just as heavy, just as light.

—Franz Kafka

The gods keep changing, but the prayers stay the same.

—Yehuda Amichai

Before a war breaks out, it has long begun in the hearts of the people.

—Leo Tolstoy

OVERLORD

OTHER

For a long time I used to love the word *now*. I murmured its
tiniest of songs to myself as a child when alone. *Now now now*
now I sang, not much knowing where we were. Until, before I knew it,
it put forth its liquid melody, and time, shimmering, began to flow
nearly inaudible, alongside the crickets if it was summer, alongside the penumbral
clock if it was the kitchen, alongside the tapping of the wintered lilac's branches on the

violet-shadowed

walls that held the garden,
if it was wind. Where were we, in fact? *Now now* the adults used to say
meaning pay attention, meaning the thing at hand, the crucial thing, has these
slippery sides: this *now* its one slope, this *now* its
other. The thing itself, the essential thing, is in between. Don't blink. Don't
miss it. Pay attention. It's a bullet.
All those years, before I became lost, I lived a different life.
One where you can go back. I thought each new

now, new

note, plucked from the as-yet-unpronounced, covered up a footstep

of the retreating God.

Where was it just before, I wondered, as it moved away in concentric circles
from the place the finger had triggered. *Tap tap* drummed my mother's hand
without her knowing on the kitchen table
in the dim end of afternoon. To keep away waiting. There is no
waiting. There will never be tomorrow. Nonetheless you do suddenly fall asleep, and then,
there it is again, when just as suddenly your eyes open, it floods in, and you
are full, and the song begins. One day

I woke up, I was

sick, in bed, my first time, since beginning, since beginning

school, since the becoming of my self.

I looked for the notes but walls slid in. A weight

descended. I was waiting. The first time. What age could I have been?

The house gave forth its ticking and tapping. One-time sounds occurred—a shutter

snapped,

a heavy clink where keys were dropped, the sweet dry

clack where a pinecone hits

gravel below. A mourning dove. Once. Then after a while, again, once.

What else could be inside me? That's when I heard

what makes me break this silence and speak to you this way.

I heard my name, as always, called out into the classroom as the schoolday began.

PEPPER, Jorie. I sat up. I knew what space it floated into, everyone waiting.

I heard it said the second time into the grayish morninglight

over the rows and rows of chairs, the gleaming fullness of them, empty, as children stood.

There was nothing I could do. I saw it as I heard it—"absent"—

said out into the room. Heard the silence that followed it.

Sitting up, I looked about. The tree beyond the windowpane flowed out to its bark.

It ticked out its being to its leaftips, down into its roots. *It could not be*

absent. The blue

cup on the dresser, its tiny blue stream, crabapples in bloom, one bird sitting on

the handrail of the bridge—what of it could ever retreat,

leaving only part of itself present?—or the clouds—on cup, in sky—or the tasseled

fringe of

curtain, door, wicker chair with rose-pattern pillow, saffron lampshade with cream-

brocaded border…I don't know if I cried out,

but they came running up to see what was wrong.

This is what is wrong: we, only we, the humans, can retreat from ourselves and

not be

altogether here.

We can be part full, only part, and not die. We can be in and out of here, now, at once, and not die. The little song, the little river, has banks. We can pull up

and sit on the banks. We can pull back

from the being of our bodies, we can live in a

portion of them, we can be absent, no one can tell.

DAWN DAY ONE

(Dec 21 '03)

A gunshot. The second, but the first I heard.
Then the walls of the room, streaked with first light, shot
                                        into place.
Then, only then, did my eyes open.
We come about first, into waking, as an *us*, I
think. Sometime between the first and second instant
there is still the current that carries one in
and deposits one in singleness. The body's weight is
a beaching. Back behind, or underneath: infinity
or something which has no consequence. Then consequence, which
feels like walls and the uprighting of self one has to do
in them, then the step one has to take once roused, and how it
puts one back on the walking-path one stepped off of
last night. Zeno reasoned we would
never get there. Reason in fact never gets there.
But we step back onto the path each time.
How long have you been yours, are you tired, are you
in a hurry, are you sitting down, is that stillness
still your pathway which you enter
                    now only with
your mind—which keeps on stepping mind you—
until it doesn't and the stopping
                    happens again.
Are your eyes shut? I put cream on my lids
and rub it in. I feel my eyes in there under the skin.
How impersonal are they, these hardnesses, barely

attached, in their loosely protected sacks.

Tony tells me how, in the lab, they cast an image

—a cross in this case—onto the gaze of a monkey then

"sacrifice

the monkey" and how, when examined, the neurons in the

visual cortex

actually form the imprint of

the cross. It would have been, the cross (except under very

unusual circumstances), erased

by the next image. Hence the need for

sacrifice. Of what is it made, I ask. Of cells, of *active*

cells, he says. Is it imprinted, I ask. No. It

would have disappeared and been replaced except

the creature was stilled. I like it they

use the word *stilled*. Then the back

of the cave in there with its cross of cells. Which will

dissolve as the "next instant." Some arguments

continue this way ad infinitum. And

infinitum *is* one path, but you can't

really get onto its promenade, its boardwalk, by

speculation. "Therefore" is another way to walk,

therefore the fast Achilles can never best the slow

tortoise. Zeno inferred yet another way.

And yes, now space and time can be subdivided

infinitely many times. But isn't this sad?

By now hasn't a sadness crept in?

I put my hands over both my eyes and lie

still. I think. The paradox says that you can never leave

the room in which you are right now. First walk

half the distance to the door, then half again, and so on. These eyes, under my hands, I looked at in the mirror yesterday.

Everything of course was silver, my skin, my gaze,

and then the eyes, held in

                    their lids.

Looked hard into that room.

Looked everywhere, all the way to the back. The

                              back

                            tells me

I have to come back here, here to the front, there is

no further I can go. One takes smaller and smaller steps

according to Zeno to try to leave the room. If you return now

to the glass, you can look *at* your eyes. After a short

time, very short if you hold fast, don't blink, just stare,

you will be looking at *an other*. A silver one. I promise

you, go do it now, you will see it, it is not you.

It is more exactly not-you than anyone you've

ever seen. Keep staring. Even Achilles must take

smaller and smaller steps. Even so he can never win.

Before Zeno there was Pythagoras. Before Pythagoras humans

did not understand—that is the verb that is used—that results

had to be proved. That there is an edifice

you can build, level upon level, from first principles,

using axioms, using logic. Finally you have a house

which houses you. Now look at you.

Are you an entire system of logic and truth?

Are you a pathway with no body ever really on it?

Are you shatterable if you took your fist now to

this face that looks at you as you hold to your stare?

Here. You are at the beginning of something. At the exact

beginning. Ok. This is awakening

number two in here, in this poem. Then there are
these: me: you: you *there*. I'm actually staring up at
you, you know, right here, right from the pool of this page.
Don't worry where else I am, I am here. Don't
worry if I'm still alive, you are.

PRAYING *(Attempt of June 8 '03)*

One of us is awake, not the other, it seems to me here
in the dark—also can't tell if that's the radiator or the first
birds—the young soldier is once again being admitted
to hospital so they can repair him and return him to the theatre,
to make what *operational?*—why—why am I awake, or is it you, not me, that
is—if Orion had something in his pocket, it would fall out
over the house you said in your sleep, but it was true, I went
and looked, why is it so terrifying Orion's still here, this late in
the story, hunting all night, pack of hounds all over the sky,
also prey all over the sky, sometimes his prey *by accident* being his

                                      beloved

hounds, yes—is it that we cannot tell each other apart, so we have to

                                     make up

something that will count as difference—*real* difference—how
different does it have to be, the difference, to count, to do its job
trying as it is to save us, or so history would have us believe—
and if I look now into that black up there am I to see

                            its point—

or now, from the as-yet-invisible marshes, where there's a shot, where the men

                            of Trevieres are

                            spending this night in

blinds, hunting, there, another shot,
where the children-turned-into-men of aligned and un-
aligned nations are making their treaties, taking their booty, all night—
declarations of loyalty floating in the air they are

                         breathing—ever more

                         toxic, barely sustainable—where

these yet more humans, pushed out, hard, into this, by mothers

screaming, this

passage of time

in which they now stand, aiming up into the air before dawn,

right up at those too still stars

scoured earlier-on by now dead boys, desperate, in these same marshes, hiding,

listening hard for

the enemy, for its tiniest sounds, listening

all night long, exhausted—strays from the 116th—

having all been dragged by riptide up to Dog Green (Omaha)

whereas they had been meant to meet H hour, miles away, down at Dog Red (still

Omaha)—

others meant for Easy Green or Easy Red also thrown at Dog—mostly all still

alive—off-schedule—including the

sweepers—all dragged down, freezing, waves huge—*meant* to land

where gun emplacements were less thick and channels between lines

of tracer-fire

could be *read through* the surface of

the beach

because mercifully the guns

could not be rotated

so much as an inch,

such that the stitchery of fire, once tracked on sand, or on

successive rows of flesh, lets you

gauge-out, for just a flash—if you

are someone granted that cracked

flash, two seconds, maybe three, of life—the

passage through—[there it is, the word *mercy*][me shooting

the very sound up now

with faulty weapon]["Now in my glass appears/

the soldier who is going to die./He smiles and moves about in ways/

his mother knows. I cry

NOW"]. Are you awake, I listen for your breathing here,

I am beside myself, I am beside these words, as close

to *it* as I can be, not close enough though, not by a long shot, oh god

won't you leave us alone, you've got us half scared to death—outside, all round, fog,

"freedom,"

through which the soldiers and the hunters wade, heavy mist—

and there, again now, a shot—a hit or miss—how easy it is to make a ghost—

as here, don't you see, the minute I stop scribbling here

I will be gone—truth is a collective event—no that's not what he

said, he said

truth is a collective error—the spirit does or does not die

with the body, that being maybe the only real question left us,

besides "us," the other great mystery, whether any one of us

can even touch an other one of us, even here, naked, trying to get back

to sleep, chairs and tables

pushing out void, taking up room, *I tell it*

as I see it says the young man holding the gun, while I

keep counting my numbers out—when will I have enough

to make it through, to fall asleep—as now again I

have to start over

where a shot from out there shatters

my count... Strange how the number drops out of mind.

As when I counted the stars, long nights, in childhood, out.

Loud tiny voice. So adamant, stern. Up into the hundreds, many

hundreds. Each star. Held firm. First in eye, then in mind. Then suddenly,

terrible, losing my place—ghastly, spilling, whole night sky

unraveling—and *where* was I reaching, panicky, trying to catch the outermost

number, the one I

just had—where was I—where is it—oh lord it is a

        small thing, no?, to have to

        begin the count

again—the stars, the butterflies, the flies, the scars,

the dead, the rooms, the sand, the words, the wounded, the roads, the missing limbs,

                              the *whose*

of the missing limbs, the missing, the starlings, the prayers, the in-

dividual secrets, the bullets, the days, from the beginning again, the

days. Start counting. Too much blood. Under the bridge.

Start. Start putting things back. To still us. Start.

SOLDATENFRIEDHOF

(German Cemetery, La Cambe, Normandy, 2003,
Computer Terminal)

"To find a fallen person," it says, "push green key."
Fill in name, last name, first name, I put in
Klein. 210 Kleins in the Soldatenfriedhof.
I scroll. Klein stays the same.
The first name changes, rank, row, plot.
No. The graveyard changes too. At 88 Klein's in
Colleville (US graveyard). At 93 he's in the British one (Bayeux).
Have you found your fallen person says the program
when I go back to the home page. No slot for
nationality. None for religion. Just date of
                              birth,
then rank, row, plot, and field come forth. I'm staring at
                              the soundless
screen. Keys very large for easy use.
Back through the doorway there's the
field. 21,222 German soldiers. Some named, some not.
Inside the office now a wide face looking up.
When is the last time a new man was found, I ask.
Here it is full, he says, people now go to Saint André.
So there are no new bodies being found?
Oh no. No, no. Just last month eight—
here look, pulling a red file from a stack.
Look—and it's open—here, you'll see.
A name, a question mark, a print of teeth of which two

(lost after death) marked "lost after death." A plastic

baggie holds an oval metal tag, almost

illegible, now placed into

my hand. The other baggie he snaps open: here:

a button: we mostly tell them from the buttons:

this was a paratrooper: you can see from

the size, the color of the casing. The sleeve

of something other than time, I think,

slides open to reveal, nested, as in a pod, this seed, hard, dark, how does he

make out its

identity—a paratrooper—a German one—each people's

buttons different—if it's a German, we get called—if he is ours

we begin work—whatever clothing still exists—part of

a boot,

a lace, can get you back

the person—a metal clip—the stitching of a kind of

cloth. There were so many kinds of fiber then. Then

as much soil as we can get—bone-fragments when there are—

how fast flesh turns to soil again—that is why clothing is

so good.

Where there are teeth too it is good—

we will be able to notify the family.

There is great peace in knowing your person is found.

Mostly in Spring when the land is plowed.

Sometimes when they widen roads.

Many were put in with the apple trees.

One feels, from the way they are placed, the burying

was filled with kindness. I don't really know why, but it is

so. I turn the oval in my hand. Soil on it still, inside the chiseled number-

group, deeper

in the 3's and 8's, so that it's harder to make out the whole.

The boy is 17 he says.

What if he hadn't been found.

What if he is now found.

What does he re-enter.

Saint André de Champigny will receive

some earth, jaw, teeth, buttons, dog-tag, an

insignia, hair, bones of most of one

right hand. When more than one have been found

together, the official of the graves registration department

—this man with soft large hands holding the folder out—

portions out enough human remains

to make up as many people as possible.

The possible person: a tooth is enough. *Anything*

will do

really, he says looking up, almost inaudibly.

With whom is he pleading.

Behind him now the field where in 1947 American bodies, and parts-of, put here

temporarily,

were dug up and moved for the final time

to their last resting place, to the American Normandy War Memorial—

and these available German parts and wholes pulled from their

holding grounds and placed in openings Americans

released.

Forgive me says the man still in his seat,

I have been rude, I did not mean (gets up)

my name is _____, here is my card.

May I hold the button a moment longer?

You from under the apple orchard,

you still not found in my field,

and the mole hacking through,
and the rabbits at dawn eating,
and the bird I cannot identify,
you, meaninglessness,
speak out—what do you hate—what do you hate—

PRAYING *(Attempt of June 6 '03)*

I wake and one of them is still there, still talking, sudden jolts of hand

as if to

slap open the

air, garbage waiting at the curb, myself a slave, still, yes, I check, a
slave, mist on the hedgerows, stubblefields between. A slave. Beyond,
the village still asleep. That I can say the word *village.* Thorns
disappearing now under the last of the blossoming.
God why do so many of your plants have thorns.
Yesterday, along the roads, looking up, but barely, as I passed,
people collecting something edible from the edges of the ditches.
Strangeness envelops me. I know I too am dying but I don't say that
here. Why? Why does even the use of the question mark seem too
pronounced for the way it feels. Once an angel cried out.
Once "once" had a long tail, time went backwards and also
forwards, and the crisp shadows of the roses on the wall
made all the sense I needed to live by. There were, also,
seasons. Yes I know, there still are seasons, but you also know
we're not sure. Others are sure, they provide data, the experts
do what they wish with it and the rest is lies.
Oh but the thieves are beautifully presented, waving, getting on and off
their planes. Unlike my dream, they have all the time in
the world, waving as they descend the fore stairs, or the aft,
as no one is shooting at them. The cat we found in the hedgerow in the rain
is watching me do this. The cat has AIDS. The vet says "unfortunately
very common now." It is also very smart and beautiful. We have no
name for it. It seems that many more people are being killed by us
than they are telling us. I try to imagine the war. Someone in it

who always takes his hat off the hook, however short the trip outside, who goes

out "now"

very suddenly, to see what the noise is, and then later someone else
seeing the hat. How the hat has become unbearable.
Still the voices do not go away. Every morning now I am putting these words down
in the place of other words. Over them. In order to cover them
up. The cat this morning, because something, as we were told to expect, is starting to

go wrong,

is scratching and scratching at the hard floor to cover up a trace
of what she has not done. I pick her up to calm her but she pulls away
and goes back to what looks, to my species, like shame, the work of the
ashamed. I feel there is nowhere to turn. I watch her and believe she is growing
blind, possibly, or an hysteria is beginning to set in. I feel there is nowhere
to turn. I have borrowed money. I have borrowed faith. I have borrowed
words, style, thoughts, obedience. I have borrowed the smile,
I have borrowed the still moonlit field, the hoarfrost glowing in it, borrowed
the phone, called the number listed, called the other number, also
borrowed one person's name, then another's, also gave one name to a newborn
person. I have tried to understand the messages. I have tried to take them
back. I do not know where back is. I have searched everywhere this I can
promise you. There is no excrement but she is trying to cover it
everywhere. Her claws make a horrible sound on the stone floor as she tries.
No no there is nothing there you have done nothing I say. It is some other
species. The compartment of species-distinction I'm in slides its small door
shut. There are people who need ammunition right now or it will be

too late.

There are people

whose names are being typed onto a paper right now. One is on his
hands and knees and cannot find his voice to say please, for which
he might be killed. There is the category of by mistake for just about

everything especially death. There are people who need a driver's license or they

shall not

stay in the country. There are people who if the rent is not paid this month
shall not stay in the country. There are people who if they take something
which their child needs, or does not need, which they shall not have the

money for

shall not stay in the country. A country: I beg You, it is not Your dawn yet

here, tell me

what that is. I cannot make out what borders are. What they express is not clear
to me. Why we needed to cut it up like this. No,
it is not clear. From the hedgerows outside some are still audible.
Every morning like this with the mists on them the wide
impassable hedgerows speaking. I turn the news on only to cover it. To cover
the cat's claws scratching at the floor I have now cleaned again. To show her it is
clean. "Clean" I say stroking and pointing. Above or below us it must be all right—

is it just in our

stratum? We have tried to cover it with volume, it is still space. We have
covered it with history, it is still a murder and a forgetting. The dead are still
mixed in with the living. Maybe by mistake. Whose? The battle lines
are setting in. Everyone is in his or her hole or should be. Wherever you have
fallen, stay. Distance is your friend, covet it. Even from God, I think, for
now. Your god might be the wrong one for the circumstances.
Make yourself a kind of silence, don't say what you think.
If you decide I shall say what I please know you are putting
your loved ones at risk. Listen to the hinges, listen hard. If you care to know
what I think, I think they are robbing us blind and we want to stay
blind. Speechless too, even our loved ones will testify against us. And by

the way,

god of the absolute blind spot, unblinking,
throwing back the gates savagely to allow entry, waiting for each one of

your sons

to step out from the others, everything about him visible, his standing there

the only thing you cannot take from him, plus his silence, although you

are also making him *unable to cry out*—[what is it you are doing to his

                                                voice]—

making him yours absolutely if you can—why, lord of the

human eye, tongue, hand—of lateness—of there being such a thing as

lateness—[in relation to what]—why is it we are supposed to love? On account of

                                                its perfect

obedience, matter deserves to be loved, Weil says. Matter she says is

entirely passive and in consequence entirely obedient to God's will. I am God's

matter, says the voice from the just-greening eight-foot hedgerows. I was.

The only choice given to men, she says, is to desire obedience or not to

desire it. If a person does not desire it, he obeys nevertheless,

perpetually, inasmuch as he is a thing subject to mechanical necessity. If he does

desire it, he is still subject, but a new necessity is added, a

necessity belonging to supernatural things. It is nearing seven. When we have

                                                the feeling,

she says, that we have disobeyed God, it simply means that for a time

we have ceased to desire obedience. I desire obedience. I do not have that

towards which to direct my desire. It is a beautiful moonlit night.

The young owl that sang out once might sing again.

UPON EMERGENCE

Have I that to which to devote my
self? Have I devotion? The shoes, the
clothes? The drowning of appetites, as the chariots
were drowned? I sit at the very edge
of the garden, paying out my attention.
The moving and moving of the mottled interminable
forms—the deepness in the unseen, the
different deepnesses in the lisping way the gaze
takes time to alight. Nothing is solid as itself—
that too. A style to the visible world which is—yes like
death—but also like a spume, or the way music seems to formulate
words—a style which I can feel slip free of
point of view and gaze, the artificer mind
making explicit what is not—as in the version of a place
                                        inside a place. Is it a
future that I see? Right here, just underneath this rock I
lift—brood of tiny helmets going everywhere towards defeat—is it
sunlight laying itself hard
on the geranium leaves—which it also
fattens—an existent thing, the sun, yes, and yet, if so, *where*
does it exist? The fine hairs on the geranium leaves stand up
and catch the light. If you bend close you'll see the
future there—do you remember? "Do you re-
member" is that what devotion says? Do not forget to
remember. I feel, inside, a fantastic pressing of blood against
this skin. I hold my open hands up, here,
before my face, I listen hard to them.
Clouds press. The passings of their shadows press

onto each palm. There is no underneath.

It is all souvenir.

The bird that was just feeding here

is now appearing in my mind. The blood

inside me now must take it round and round. Hardly changed,

it bends and pecks at the last bits of seed below

the lavender. Riding on the blood in me,

its wings spread out. And also bloody, yes, the grass

of mind, bright red its stalks. Also glints on its claws, its

wingtips rising up, above the streams—of me? in me?—

borne round and round by my sticky devotion here, my *thinking* it....

So this is the source of evil? Of course I know

how small it is. But what lies buried at the core

of this holding-in-mind, this final place in which we are

compelled to bury it? We live in time. It is a

holiday. All round it timelessness which will begin again,

yet still, for now, sticks to *one* time like remnant rain

after the place is solidly in place under fresh sun.

Concerning the gods I have no means.

But from this path what is it must be

seen, what must be thought and spoken of—from this,

what is it that is taken from the visible—

what is it that cannot be given back

in *any* form—which burns off—without

residue—just by coming into contact with

the verb of human inwardness? How helpless they are—

both sides—can the gods really know?—the

ineffable pain, amazement, thronging drift

of accident whereby freedom of world, of

subject, are forced to give way? Oh

"path of inquiry"! All of it unable to die

or kill. Also unable to stay calmly under-
neath, or *in* any arrival place—no hell, even,
no hell....I know it is only the visible world.
But nothing is small enough to escape us.
Can I devote myself to setting it free?
Where, where is it free? Before I think it,
what is its state? And if I summon it
to mind, if I begin to summon it? Unbearable

tyranny. Tiny

monster picking up the reins of my eyes.
The chariots of the sun "says" the tiniest god (definition).
Beyond whispers the hillside, the paragraph
break, the insuck of breath before this
rest. *Where is your brother* hisses the page.

LITTLE EXERCISE

The screen is full of voices, all of them holding their tongues.
Certain things have to be "undergone," yes.
To come to a greater state of consciousness, yes.

Let the face show itself through the screen.
Let the organizing eyes show themselves.
Let them float to the surface of this shine and glow there.

The world now being killed by its children. Also its guests.

An oracle?—a sniper, a child beater, a dying parent in the house,
a soil so overfed it cannot hold a root system in place?
Look—the slightest wind undoes the young crop.

Are we "beyond salvation"? Will you not speak?
Such a large absence—shall it not compel the largest presence?
Can we not break the wall?
And can it please *not be a mirror* lord?

PRAYING *(Attempt of May 9 '03)*

I don't know where to start. I don't think my face

in my hands is right. Please don't let us destroy

Your world. No *the* world. I know I know nothing. I know I

can't use you like this. It feels better if I'm on

my knees, if my eyes are pressed shut so I can see

the other things, the tiniest ones. Which can still escape

us. Am I human. Please show me mercy. No please show

a way. If I look up all the possibility that you

might be there goes away. I need to be curled up this

way, face pressed, knees pulled up tight. I know

there are other ways, less protected, more expressive of

surrender. But here I can feel the whole crushing

emptiness on my back. Especially on my shoulders.

I thought just now how that emptiness could be my wings.

That you were there, maybe, laughing. That the room above me,

here, before dawn, its two windows black, this

pillow pressed down hard against me, how it, how all of it,

made up the wings. There is a reason I

have to go fast. Have to try to slide into

something I can feel the beginning of. Right

here in my pushed-down face. Right

where eyes are pressed

so sleep doesn't go there anymore.

And the mirror—well that is another way if you wish. If you

look in for a very long time. But here, I did this other thing

again. (Here)(I write the open parenthesis, press my face,

try again, then lift, close)(then this clause to explain)

(to whom?)(always wanting to be forgiven)(not seen)(no)—See,

it is already being lost here, the channel is filling

in, these words—ah—these, these—
how I don't want *them* to be the problem too, there are
so many other obstacles, can't these be just a part of
my body, look (put my head down again)(am
working in total dark)(maybe this will not be
legible)—my ears covered to go further—maybe
if I had begun otherwise, maybe if I had
been taught to believe in You, I needed evidence,
others seem not to need it, they do not seem to me
graced, but yesterday when I asked Don he said yes, he
was sure, yes,
everything was His plan, so it is a lapse of faith
to worry, you will have noted I cannot say "Your
plan," and now, as if dawn were creeping in, the
feeling of the reader is coming in, the one towards which
this tilts, like the plant I watched a long time yesterday the
head of, and then the stem itself,
to see if it turned towards the light as the light arrived,
I would say it did, very slightly, and I
could not *see it*,
though I never lifted my gaze, and tried very hard to blink only
when physically impossible not to, and yes, yes, in the end it
was in a different direction, I had marked where we started
so I knew for sure, although of course I know nothing, I could
begin this story anywhere, maybe I will open my
eyes now, although I have gotten nowhere and will
find myself
still just here, in the middle of my exactly given years, on
my knees naked in my room before dawn, the pillow
wet of course but what of it, nothing nothing comes of it,
out there where the
garbage truck will begin any second now, where I

can feel the whitening reefs (which

I have only read about)(if that means anything)(yes/no) under there where

they are,

the waters filtering through them, the pH wrong, the

terrible bleaching occurring, the temperature, what

is a few degrees, how fine are we supposed

to be, I am your instrument if you would only use me, a

degree a fraction of a degree in the beautiful thin

water, flowing through, finding as it is meant to *every*

hollow, and going in, carrying its devastation in, but looking so

simple, and a blue I have never seen, with light still in its

body as light is in mine here I believe, yes,

light a chemical analysis would reveal,

something partaking of the same photons

in this pillow, this paint on the wall, this wall,

which if I open my eyes will be five inches from my face,

which (the coral reefs having caverns) I try to go into—

because I can make myself very small is that a gift from you,

I think it might be one of the great gifts, that I can *make*

myself very small and go in, in from this room, down into the

fibrous crenellations of the reef, which if you look close are formed

by one node clipping onto an other, and then

the rounding-up as the damage occurs, as the weight is lost, now the coral

in with the

trucks, pipeknock kicking in, it is beginning

again—oh—when I open my eyes I see two white lines,

vertical, incandescent, I will keep all the knowledge

away I think, I try to think, I will keep

the knowing away, the lines seem to come out of nowhere,

they do not descend nor do they rise,

just gleam side by side in the small piece of glance

my two eyes hold in their close-up

vision. There is a flood. There are these two lines.

Then the sun moves up a notch, though still in the in-

visible, and I see, I see it is the 12-ounce glass, its body

illumined twice, white strokes where the very first

light has entered, here, I look again, it seems to gleam, it

gleams, it is the empty glass.

OMAHA

(Lowest Tide, Coefficient 105, Full Moon)

You can enlarge your soul but it is to receive what?

Did you say the thing they were expecting you to say?

Well then, see, how easy it is to be somebody else.

Like someone you see who looks like yourself in a dream,

for instance. What is it you look like. Your face,

is it there in your hands now, or down in the water?

If in the water, can you still pick it up, put it back on,

or is that trick lost? Reflect. Quick. Have you that vacancy

                                    in you

which can be forced to collaborate?

Have you that vacancy which can be occupied,

and by what, and for how long, and at what

cost. Oh speak. Say TAKE YOUR MEDICINE.

Or PRETEND YOU DON'T KNOW WHAT IT'S ALL

ABOUT. Or whatever else it is you would have us

know. MY HOW YOU'VE GROWN would be ok,

but I'm not 'sure how you'd mean us to take that.

TAKE THAT. WHO ARE THOSE THERE.

Everything looks suddenly frighteningly reassuring.

As if the gods were rummaging through their drawers for this brief

spell, which feels like rain to us, so one can imagine

humming a little song, nothing, for just this tiny interval,

behind one's back. But look, even as we feel free

to live as if in their absence, for just this little while,

look how our mania continues to strut, oblivious. Ours,

in spite of us. What is this we are?

Even the balconied gods have their limits.

Tolerance. Boredom. One comes out to the edge now with a blue

                                        wand,

I look up. Don't draw too close.

Do you think she has a different power? She waves

the thing. Others scamper away as she reaches the rail

and leans out over us. Waves and waves of blue

seem to scatter from the tip of her wand. "You

are fools" is said by the waves, but in another tongue.

"Anaesthetized by greed" is also let loose.

Some among us think they rise triumphant by just

drawing the next breath. As I tell you this

the stage grows very dark, I can hardly make her out.

The perspective is that of an American city, where one

is peering from street level to an unfindable upper floor.

A noisy place where it seems all of this

should have been long obvious to us from the start.

When "good" and "evil" had fresh paint on them,

performing for us on their various pedestals,

and you, you could look into any store window

and see the offspring of the two

right there, dead center, from any sidewalk,

a certain resemblance to some actor—waves now, waves rolling

                                        eternally,

of men, some dead, some still alive, being swept in, being rammed in—

Agency! What is that? The drowned wash in to receive

their bullets, the living wash in to receive

theirs. They cannot really be told

apart. Not from up there where the firing originates.

Not from up there where it's a scene in a movie.

There never was an alternative.

No one after a point could have stood up and walked

         away

in fear. No. No fear. Not anymore. These are the givens:

        poverty, greed, un-

expectedness. The bubble of the *now* being emitted from the

          blossoming

then. That's all. Maybe disappearance—as of the moon

to the horror of the men already in dark.

And always the one, far away, sitting charred and absent-

minded, on his throne. And always an audience

for all this slaughter and laughter—

"later on." The last few decades at any given moment

a leaf that drops. Some twig left

bare. The change upon us. But the fall—the falling

        of it

even after it's done—the fall: continues.

Because there is no way to get the killing to end.

PRAYING *(Attempt of June 14 '03)*

This morning before dawn no stars I try again.

I want to be saved but from what. Researchers in California have

discovered a broken heart causes as much distress

in the pain center of the brain as physical injury.

The news was outside the door on the landing. I

squatted to it then came back in. Resume my

position. Knees tight, face pressed. There seems to be

a canyon. No light in it, yet it's there, but then

nothing. *Waste* comes

in, I know they are

burying our waste, that it will last hundreds of millions

of years in the mountain, that they are trying to cover it with signs they

do not know how to develop in

a language that will still communicate in that far

future saying don't open this, this is lethal beyond

measure, back away, go away, close the lid, close

the door. The canyons where my face lies full weight on the platter

of my hands have ridges and go forward only to

the buried waste. If there is beauty growing on those

flanks, beauty in detail—furred underside

of small desert leaves comes to mind but only as idea—

the sage twiggy stuff with its blue flowers—the succulent

floor plants that rise—the hundreds of crossing mucus-tracks on the walls where the

snails have been

guiding the first light

down their slick avenues to some core—all of it *just in*

mind not on my closed face trying

so hard to let the thing that can save us in—if

there is beauty it is missing in its manyness is only there

in form I am trying to be honest I am not relying on

chance any more I am trying to take matters

into my own hands. Hand heart head.

Brain pain center sleep. I try to

remember. Something that *was* once is not graspable

from here. Here is all here. Is the problem. Have

tucked the body away. Am all alone on this

floor. In a city in America. To make a

sacrifice. Of what. Save my beloveds. Save my

child. Save her right now. Destroy this carpeting these

windows the walls take the whole of what is wrong

in payment from us. Let me fall through the air.

Save the will to live, save the constituent part of

the human. No. What is constituent. Oh

save my child, my only child.

The more I press down onto the rug the more we move up the

canyon. In Mycenae we moved up this canyon too,

up, up through the city to the throne room at the top.

The columns still standing. The view of two oceans and over two

ranges. Where the King and his retinue are receiving the news. Here. The

poet ushered in. To sing of what has happened. Right here.

On this floor. The voice telling its story. Long, slow, in detail. All of them

waiting. Listening for the terrible outcome. In detail. The opening

of the singer at the throat. The still bodies of the

listeners, high on this outpost, 3,000 years ago, the house of

Agamemnon, the opening of the future. There. Right through the open

mouth of the singer. What happened, what

is to come. And the stillness surrounding them when it is done,

the song. And the singer still. And the chalices empty.

Dawn about to open it all up again. Dawn about to

move it from inside the mind back out. Light almost visible
on the far hills. Oh who will hear this. When it comes it will be time only for
action. Keep us in the telling I say face to the floor.
Keep us in the story. Do not force us back into the hell
of action, we only know how to kill. Once we stop singing we
only know how to get up and stride out of the room and begin
to choose, this from that, this from that, this from that,—and the pain,
the pain sliding into the folds of the brain and lodging.

Look, the steps move us up through the dark, I can hear them
even though I can't see them, we are moving further up,
this that this that and the pain sliding all along,
sliding into the fine crevices on the side walls of this brain we are
traveling up, and the pain lodging, and the pain finding the spot of
                                        unforgetting,

as in here I am, here I am.

SPOKEN FROM THE HEDGEROWS

I was Floyd West (1st Division) I was born in Portia Arkansas Feb 6
1919 We went through Reykjavik Iceland through the North Atlantic through the
                                                                    wolf packs
That was 1942 I was Don Whitsitt I flew a B-26 medium bomber
Number 131657 called the Mississippi Mudcat I was a member of

The 387th Bomb Group and then later the 559th Bomb
Squadron. Picked up the Mudcat in Mt. Clemens Michigan
Flew over our whole group four squadrons sixteen planes each
from Hunter Field at Savannah Georgia then to Langley Field at

Norfolk Virginia from there to Grenier Field at Manchester New Hampshire
In each place stayed a day or two
From Grenier went on to port of embarkation
which was Presque Isle, Maine, then started across, first to Goose Bay, Labrador,

then to Bluie West One, Greenland, then over the cap to
Mick's Field, Iceland. Made landfall at Stornoway, Scotland, from there
down to Prestwick, north London, finally Station 162 at Chipping
Ongar. My name was Dan, 392nd Squadron of the 367th Fighter Group

March 21 boarded the *Duchess of Bedford* in NY,
an old English freighter which had been converted
to bring over the load of German prisoners, whom we replaced

going back to England. Slept below decks in hammocks.
April 3rd arrived at Scotland, and, following a beautiful trip through
the country, arrived at Stoney Cross, ten miles from the Channel—

it was a beautiful moonlit night. I was known as Bob. I was in
D Company. My number was 20364227. I was born Feb 3,
1925, Bristol, Tennessee. We embarked on the HMS

Queen Mary, stripped, painted dull gray, hammocks installed with
troops sleeping in shifts. The *Queen* was capable of making twenty-eight knots
and therefore traveled unescorted, since it could outrun any

sub. Walter, given name, 29th Division. We crossed on the *Queen Mary.* The
swimming pool was covered over, that's where most of us slept.
My name was Alan, Alan Anderson, 467th Anti-Aircraft Artillery. I was given

birth November 1, 1917, Winchester, Wisconsin. They took us to
Fort Dix for England. We took the northern route in the extreme rough sea of
January. It was thought that this would confuse the

German subs. It didn't exactly work that way.
A convoy ahead of us by a few days was hit, many ships sank.
I saw the bodies of so many sailors and soldiers floating by us

with all the other debris and ice on the water. The name given me
was John, born September 13, '24, in Chattanooga, but raised
in Jacksonville. I was a person, graduated high school in '42,

crossed over on the *Ile de France,* a five-decker, ten thousand on board.
They loaded over twenty on the *Queen Mary*
there on the other side of the pier. My name was Ralph, Second Class Pharmacist's Mate,
July 4 received orders to Norfolk. There's no describing

crossing the Atlantic in winter. We couldn't stay in our bunks

without being strapped in and fastened to metal pipes on
each side. We had one meal a day. My name, Robert, was put to me

in Atchison, Kansas, United States, August 15, 1916, year of the

Lord we used to figure on, there, in the 149th Engineer Combat Battalion,
which arrived Liverpool, England, January 8 1944. It rained every day.
From there we were taken to the town of Paignton. The authorities

would go down the road, and the truck would stop, and they'd say
"All right, three of you out here" and they'd march you to a house and say to
the owner,
"all right, these are your Americans. They are going to be staying with you."

SPOKEN FROM THE HEDGEROWS

[H-Hour—146 Minutes]

Keokuk was to be the first daylight mission using only the big wood
                                        gliders, the
"english coffins"— good weather all the way to
France—squadrons of Americans flying cover—seven minutes early our being
                                        cut
loose—enemy having by then almost a full day's
                    experience of
us—St. Come du Mont—Turqueville—so this time not firing on the tow—this
                                        time
holding their fire, letting us pass over—we pass over—unloading then,
                                only then, into
us—us slowly descending—one shot taken by a
knee, bullets up through our feet, explosion of Jack's face, more sudden openings
in backs, shoulders, one in a neck, throat opens, I happen to see, I see an eye
pushed back, through the face, then on back through
the canvas skin, below can see
the ones just ahead of us skidding into huge rapid
trees, see fracturing of the wooden fuselage, impaling of the
men. Howitzers and jeeps fly into the
landscape. Crates of grenades.
Yet the weather over the Channel very good.
Excellent visibility. What are we all listening
                    for, it seems we
                    are all
listening. Holding our weapons in front of us.
Told to wait. Waiting. Release altitude 750 feet. Re-
                                lease takes

place. Gliding. Miles of silence. More.

Unknown to us release point

turns out to be directly over enemy strongpoint.

The tow alone takes 600 rounds.

We have neither darkness nor surprise to help us.

Shrapnel lacerates the canvas skins.

Equipment tears into bodies.

If a man jumps to the aid of his fellow

he unbalances the already wobbly craft.

Helmets flying everywhere. All round us pilots

aiming straight-in for crash landings.

Someone is shouting: escape from wreck, seek

cover, wait in the nearest ditch till dark.

But we are slaughtered in our seats.

Holding on to our rifles we are all slaughtered. The bullets burst up

through our boots. Heavy wind hits.

Scraps of canvas hang and slap

against the glider's tubular frame.

From next to the farmhouse, snipers empty their rifles into us.

The glider missions will continue tomorrow as scheduled.

I do not know who I am, but I am here, I tell you this.

[H-Hour]

Over the field, over the one still-active radio, President Roosevelt delivers

his Prayer

to the World: *Almighty God: our sons, pride of our nation, our religion,*

and our

civilization, have set upon a mighty endeavor,

to set free a suffering humanity. Give strength, stoutness, steadfastness.
Success may not come with rushing speed. But we shall return
again and again. We know, by the grace and righteousness of

our cause, our sons will triumph.
They fight to liberate. They fight to let justice rise
among all Thy people. Some will never return.

Embrace these, Father, and receive them,
Thy heroic servants, into Thy Kingdom.
Fields heard what they could. Day heard what it could.

I do not know why I speak to you. I too
heard what I could.

SPOKEN FROM THE HEDGEROWS

To bring back a time and place.
A feeling. As in "we are all in this
together." Or "the United States and her allies

fought for Freedom." To bring back.
The experience of killing and getting killed.
Get missed. Get hit. Sun—is it with us. Holiday,

are you with us on this beach today.
Hemisphere of one, my soul, paratrooper,
greatness I house in my body, deepset, my

hands on these triggers—who once could outrun
his brother—consumed with fellow-feeling like a madness that does not,
                                                              must not,
lower its pitch—going to the meeting place,

the spire of the church in Vierville, seen on aerial maps, visible from
                                              eighteen miles out,
if it weren't for fog, and smoke, and groundmist,
the meeting place, the appointed time surging in me,

needing to be pierced—but not me—not me—

only those to the left and right of me—

permit me to let you see me—

Me. Driven half mad but still in biography.
By the shared misery of. Hatred. Training. Trust. Fear.
Listening to the chatter each night of those who survived the day.

There is no other human relationship like it.
At its heart comradeship is an ecstasy.
You will die for an other. You will not consider it a personal

loss. Private Kurt Gabel, 513 Parachute Infantry Regiment—
"The three of us Jake, Joe and I became an entity.
An entity—never to be relinquished, never to be

repeated. An entity is where a man literally insists
on going hungry for another. A man insists on dying for
an other. Protect. Bail out. No regard to

consequence. A mystical concoction." A last piece
of bread. And gladly. You must understand what is meant by
gladly. All armies throughout history have tried

to create this bond among their men. Few succeeded as well
as the paratroop infantry of the U.S. Army,
Rifle Company E, 506th.

Fussell: It can't happen to me. It can happen to me. It is
going to happen to me. Nothing
is going to prevent it.

Webster (to his parents): I am living on borrowed time—

I do not think I shall live through the next jump.
If I don't come back, try not to take it too hard.

I wish I could persuade you to regard death
as casually as we do over here. In the heat of it
you expect it, you are expecting it, you are not surprised

by anything anymore, not surprised when your friend
is machine-gunned in the face. It's not like your life, at home,
where death is so unexpected. (And to mother):

would you prefer for someone else's son to die in the mud?
And there is no way out short of the end of war or the loss
of limb. Any other wound is patched up and you're sent back

to the front. This wound which almost killed him
healed up well and he went back.
He never volunteered. One cannot volunteer.

If death comes, friend, let it come quick.
And don't play the hero, there is no past or future. Don't play
the hero. Ok. Let's go. Move out. Say goodbye.

DISENCHANTMENT

(Gerhard Richter)

*

How one wants to be other than "being." How one wants to be a kind of
$$\text{flagellation—a}$$
genuine hearing—listen—that whisper, that whistling "over there"—are we just in time?
So blank. So open to the brushwork of
$$\text{the given.}$$
That it spill its strokes onto us—build itself upon us—holy garment—("a life").
Is it all coming nearer? Are we ripening?
Is this, finally, the hoped-for undrowning of the self—a final "yes"—awash in childhood
$$\text{(whizzing past),}$$
and silence [so intense] and us no wiser for it,
and the new feeling of *the thing* inside one—
flooded with duration—sort of silvery...
Then it was time to go to the opening.
That was the end of the first day.

*

"I want this to be seen—listen to me—always—as a narrative—
even if it is a narrative of nothingness—nothing is something—you might
$$\text{say, no?—}$$
as you might say these are photographs of nothing."
You can look for instance in Ensslin's corpse,
at Baader's bookshelves, the ones in prison,
or the phonograph in which Baader was said to have hidden the gun
with which he killed himself—here: Meins surrendering

to the police—here: two versions of Baader's corpse—

head, face and floor like adjacent clouds, grayish—

the whole drama [history] floating by over the bodies, yes—

an aggressive weapon, but also a plan of defense?—

the moment in which you give yourself away?—

the stroke of midnight, say—*that* moment—[it

                being all over]—

and you, you who have the means of keeping it,

of not turning to dust, right here in front of me, of not letting it

                        turn to dust—

[I can't make you, of course, he says, I can only copy you]

[here in my garden, dreaming of becoming complicated]—[the contract between us

                          freely drawn up, but

                          not "free"]—[as you

                          know]—

[end of the second] and yet

                        *

all in vain, the things *themselves* turning to dust—

reducing this world to just this world—

the copier still here, at this dinner table, waiting for the meal to be over—

the words "after all" suddenly important—

"after all, all things are possible in a certain way are they

not?"—the madness of non-discovery cloaking you gently, brightly—

long may it prosper, the dream of transparency—

the "succession of events," the scene that takes on the "feeling of

distance." Or my asking "can anybody in here read this page"—

Oh private words, certainty, profit, manners,

this looking-away that we've come to call knowledge.
Even this crumb, here, full of echo, wanting to mean.
Invented for that purpose—little brilliant phoneme—what is transparency
to your echoing *now?* The fullness of what is given? The stroking of
[where the third day closes]

*

the ever-receding last analysis [*a life*]—into which being cannot but
enter [yes]—[*I wanted to paint nothing, how is it*
I cannot paint nothing?]—is it still the only garden? And us
                                 eternally foreigners?
                                       Perhaps *you*
can look into the vanishing "point": perhaps the father was the father, for
                                                       instance,
the mother didn't really know [here the painter pauses, before revealing something
else]: she was in a mixed-class, mismatched relationship, she had taken
another lover by the end of the war, she made him feel special, he was special, she
fostered his sense of social superiority, but he has few warm memories, they died,
it was not really possible for me to go back [he says matter of factly] [then returns
                                       to his dinner]. Stroke of
luck [brushes stacked in drawers, custom-designed, rolling
shelves] [when your work sells for] [millions of dollars] [you] [can]
indulge yourself. You can paint to prove that painting is dead. You can
paint as a true believer in painting. [Oh I should] [I really should] [you *said*
it was there] [truly there] [I only had to take the photograph]
[and that only one thing exists] [no... not death!] [this!] [holds up his birth
date] [on a tiny white card] [This, *this*—(picks up a photograph)]:
a snowy scene, at the edge of a building, behind some trees, leading to... [that was
                                       the fourth day]

Look now: he carries it to the edge of his studio: he puts the canvas on an easel

at the end of the room: he slides the photo into the projector:

the photo appears, projected on the canvas—[can you hear them? the poisonous

promises filtering down][Faust: don't you bare your greedy teeth at me

like that! It sickens me—Great, magnificent spirit that deigned appear to me,

that knows my heart and soul—feast, feast][Mephisto: Have you finished?]

(*song from within:* My mother, the whore,/Who has murdered me—/My father,

the rogue, /Who has eaten me—/Pick up every bone/Pick up every bone)—

beginning to trace with charcoal now, a ruler, a tracing of

                              each detail of

the photograph, as he always does, [which usually takes about

a couple of hours]["I have an eye. I couldn't make

a drawing of you sitting there right now. I would love to have that

ability. In the same way I would love to play the piano. But you can do

anything now, and simply declare it to be art"][his father a schoolteacher who

                                        joined

The Party, it was necessary and expected if he wanted to keep his job,

who fought in the army was taken prisoner by the Americans,

and then returned home without prospects, like so many others]

By then his son regarded him as a hapless interloper.

I thought, what do you want here.

He wasn't my father anyway.

He says he doesn't know who his real father was. He says

she had taken another lover by the end of the war.

He knows he is the greatest living artist.

Only operating rooms are this immaculate. [here ends

the fifth]

What I have is facility.

Virtuosity is important, yes,

but you have to know *when* to paint the color chart,

and *what* to call it.

You have to unmask painting as dull and nugatory

[if you are human, pity my distress]

you have to demystify the *activity* of painting and its pretensions

to creativity,

you have to love beauty, you have to say "I believe in beauty"

("and then they were very cheap, now they sell for a fortune!")

("so maybe they were therefore necessary")

with a bunch of keys and a lamp before a small iron gate:

"a long unwonted shudder grips,

mankind's entire grief grips me.

She's here, behind this wall that drips.

Do you hesitate to go in?

Do you dread to see her again?"

hears the clanking chains and the rustling straw.

[you'll awaken the guards! speak quietly!]

[Oh sleep the sleep of the end of the sixth of the days]

*

All this and morning still before us—

the snowy scene, the side of the building—its *staying,* a kind of raging, a burning of

design—

of intentions—house invented for you to hide in—have you now grown up? moved

away?—a jewel?—projected with all its weather

onto the blank canvas?—and nothing left out—nothing left hidden—

existence: is it in it? is it found hanging in its cell?—

there was to be a meeting, as one of lovers, but then something was

                                        arrested—

just there where the center was beginning to form—

no, there should not be a center—listen how it echoes—

you can blot it nicely with some abstraction—

something applied to the blank,—"gaudy and generic"—

"then he employs homemade wood and plexi squeegees"

to scam and drag the paint—[every direction the right one!]—

["I don't think you are 'expressionistic,' are you?"]

the process involves repeatedly building up and wiping off—

the effect different depending on the squeegee—on "how pressure

is applied"—he has become very adept but there is still the element of chance—

perhaps you are being kept here, somewhere in this room—

you have hidden a gun? you have hidden whatever means

you might need to get out? is your body here? is your photograph?,

[where are your hands, is it the color-chart, is it

                        the tablecloth?],

someone now removing any trace of the coffee cup

there on the table where I had just left it,

transparent guardian of all that is and could be—

Listen, in your cell, your act is the only sentinel

then there's all this construction—it is fierce yes, it will acquit no one—

distant impulses render the whole surface ultra-sensitive,

all the middle distance, the concerned elaboration—

the year x saw him joined, the year y saw him married—

and the past, the past is also yours to keep if you wish,

with its own last effort to outwit you,

with its silently projected map of the world.

[and on the seventh]:

Where the winter grew white, we went outside.
We went outside to look at things again.
There were little farmhouses, there were too many trees.
But once you have seen a thing, you have to move on.

Whose idea was this—how even when we're late now we're perfectly happy.
We just go on happily gathering speed.
Us—like a list of examples that keeps growing faster.
Embracing brutality and importance. Some joy. Some preliminary
                                                    sketches.

EUROPE *(Omaha Beach 2003)*

Walking I try to tell the plastics from the kelp—

green lettucing, wiry reds, soggy,

whitish, papery, brushing—all intermeshed—a tire track

crossing through, water still dripping downslope,

and bits of green—right here in front of me—puffing up as sun

releases them from their own weight and water is lifted

away.

A trailer tries to pull a boat upshore.

How is it that "representation" became "ornamentation."

Children as usual at work in the tidepools.

Made larger here by bits of mostly submerged landing-craft.

Now not submerged.

The tractor growing smaller as it aims towards the breakers.

Small piercing birds suddenly made audible

because of the full sound of the distant surf

now pulled across the whole—rip where

jet-skis cut and (without looking up) the single-engine

plane. What are you leaving, species of mine,

people, fuels, enemies, other—you, you there—what

for me to stand on, from which to shade my eyes and

peer. To shade and look out—long and slow—into

the "beautiful" oncoming day. When was it you last

woke to that? Yes you. I'm going closer to the

tidepools and the kids to listen and to look. One boy, maybe eight,

moves cat-like, ankle-deep,

bent over, net in hand. Whatever he has

caught he places in a bright green tub. He calls

his brother urgently in Dutch (I think) they
change the plan. The bottom of the pool is deeper and they
move towards it. They do not see me on the other side.
They're running out with buckets now, up shore, hands full.
I walk into the pool myself. Sun looks
as usual back up at me. Three
new kids are approaching now.
Green bucket has returned. He has a shovel now and
larger friend—also blond and very pale. They bend to work. Their work
makes ripples that now lap my way.
Huge kelp-pods floating from the bottom are avoided
but they sway. I barely make out numbers on
the landing-craft—barnacles, brightest of velvet greens, also a hinge,
a giant ring embedded in the deep concrete, which they
now find, and drop their buckets to climb on.
A mother calls. The bucket has been left to float. It cants
into the center of the pool where all the kelp-heads
stop. Boats, surf, cries, miles, pools, bars, war. No
container, friend. No basic building blocks "of
matter." No constituent particles from which everything
is made. No made. No human eye. The rules?
Everything speeding towards "the observer." Who is
that? The other who is me perceives
the tiny stream of particles, hazy,
the superimposition of states. Entanglement. Immediacy.
No time has passed from then. No *now.* A mother to my left
with high-pitched, lengthy reprimand. I do not speak
the tongue although I can hear rise and fall.
A ball—orange and white—is kicked my way. I
look up quickly, skip to kick it back. A small

boy running towards me startles-up, surprised. It makes him

fall. Why is he so afraid of me? Or isn't he? Why can't I

tell. Electrons hum. Photons attach

to my gaze now upon his face. Is it, his face,

a version of a possible outcome

only mathematics can explain to me?

What should I do to make him not afraid?

I watch the other children work the

ball—sand kicking up—a father in the game—

some disagreements as to where

the boundaries are.

What can I do to make him not afraid?

The electron lives in a *literally* different space.

It is called Hilbert's space.

You can't go there. It is not what we mean by

"real," but it is real. Not theoretical. Just made *entirely* of

prediction—but is real. A kind of box

made out of all of our predicted outcomes. Yet is real.

Someone *goes on* in it.

Don't seek. It is not open to seeking.

A set of rules?

Have you radical doubt?

Is there enough left to doubt about?

What must I do to make him not afraid?

IMPRESSIONISM

(near St. Laurent sur Mer)

1.

Under her bonnet the silent little girl
in a white frock whose puffed-up sleeves sputter
                in the little
wind, whose also-white pinafore slaps its looping back-bow
this way and that against the landscape, stands
             very still,
on a small, arcing, quasi-ornamental bridge over the inlet streaming
               between dunes and land.
Sun shines down hard.
Everything seems to want to shout something out.
Beyond her, on that side, dune and tall dune grasses
             juggling long winds all one way
at any given once,
        made silvery by every mile-long bend.
She's leaning on the wooden rail. Her frock is jagged in its
            private wind
of starch and straightenings and cleanliness. Her hair
is held by tiny yellow bows.

2.

Downstream blue herons, two, wade in and fish.
Each beak catches the light a little differently.
Also, once, the foot uplifts in the isosceles

of just a single wading-step—half-interrupted now, as if mid-thought.

Look how it's held

as the eye discerns, among the currents, the half-truth that can

be caught.

3.

I feel these are the tablets of the law.
Midsummer, noon, grass, sand, surf, cloth.
Rectitude of birds. In-
candescent pinafore where she leans out over the

railing now.

The parked cars gleam. The streamlet gleams.
What is it one would listen past to hear?
Hands in my pockets I think of the holy tablets
again, trying to look everywhere at once.
What more am I supposed to do.
The bottom of things is neither life nor death.
The bottom is something else.

4.

As if a tree could siphon all its swollen fruit
back in, down into its limbs, dry up the

tiny opening

where manifestation slipped out—
taking it all back in—until it disappears—until
that's it: the empty tree with all inside it still—
versus this branching-out before me of *difference*, all

brilliantly lit, out-

reaching, variegating,

feeding a massive hunger.

The heron is full of hunger.

The miles of one-thought-driven grasses full of

hunger.

Although not in this register.

5.

I feel there is only one question.

Everywhere the shine covering the *through*

through which hunger must move.

And gladly. It must be done gladly or it

will not

serve. And yes there is surplus—

but on the surface (untouchable) and in the

narrow

(inaudible) we are slaves, ferrying the hunger back and

forth.

6.

From the railing, down into the streambed,

a yellow string hangs from the fist of the

child—

crayon-yellow—fuzzy—with tiny filaments light lets us

see wind in.

It is repeated on the surface, then where it enters,

breaks.

Wind throbs sky, dress, grasses, about, but

the string's held taut by something underneath, so taut that very

close you'd hear the thrumming it is forced to make.
Perfect vertical! Calm fills me as I reach the
                                   child.
What's on your string, I ask, arms full—towels, shoes, basket and
                                        my book.

Where are the others is something that I also think.
Also how full my head is of the wind,
papery, stripping my face away—hot dry woodplanks
                                   where my feet

are placed. Let it come on.
If I stand still I see
the shadow of the string on wood
grow shorter as it's drawn back up into
its source. Soon *something* will be here. I feel
consumer confidence: I laugh
out loud. A little wind.
Birdcheeping in the tall grass now.

7.

Swollen, thick, pin-cushioned-up with fat and slack-dead open
                                   pores,
the bleached-out jumbo turkey-leg and thigh draws up
knotted to this yellow string—eleven crabs attached, all feeding
                                 wildly on their
                                   catch, clacking
their armors onto each other, claws embedded—pulled-up
                           by the yolk-
                           yellow force
onto the dock and crushed, each, at the head by the child's hammer
                               taken to them

one by one—fast—only one scrambling across the bridge today

to get away—

the leg/thigh leaking all over the fading grayed-out planks,
the full-moon catch of crabs picked up claw-end by many
hands that seem to suddenly materialize
out of the nowhere to which I am

now sent.

There's no way back believe me.
I'm writing you from there.

PHYSICIAN

My person is sick. It trembles. They have looked everywhere

in my body for a cause, oh my body is brilliant. Forgive my brilliant body, dear

gods, whatever hallway you have strayed down—maybe even answering

a house call? Maybe finding your way out? I agree

the layout is growing increasingly complicated. Not one exit is

marked. It must feel to you like a horrible labyrinth, this

history of ours. No

opening. And all our walls! Everywhere crammed full of the crushed

and confused and still-milling numberless angels.

Everywhere in the solids of our world them rushing towards each other.

As there is nowhere *else* for them to rush towards.

Even in my room, in my walls, right there, deep inside them,

something filled with greatest passion, thickening folds of it, is

                              personally embracing

                          a void.

My person, ah, America, sinks into its bed.

Into the brooding.

All day long reads only the *Physicians' Desk*

Reference. To find out what is wrong. Has *all*

the symptoms. Is not mad. Wants to tell you,

read carefully, you will find you have them

too. This takes a while, but after a while, you will find yourself

shuddering into your diagnosis. It's like having inside you

numberless confused angels. At evening my person

                      looks briefly out of

the upstairs window, just before the light goes,

over the stony valley, where the hawk always sweeps round

the left end of the field. That is YOUR field my person says under its breath, and the hawk knows it, and the disease knows it,

and the summer which is very far away and which might never

come back knows it, even the steps out the front door

which might never again give of their service

to my person know it. *Your field, yours,* it says

although this time only with its eyes, as the room stuffed full of angels is best

kept silent. My person loves history. It loves the great battles which make it weep

as it lies in bed remembering. It wants to remember all of them.

What did we look like then? The bugle boy

enters into the room, shyness in him, then the note

is sounded. A crowd of horses tries to turn around in

the small room—the bed in their way—the nightlights

confusing. Their riders have a hard time holding.

Where the hell are they? IN MY BODY'S HEART.

Formation for battle, first assault—it is not easy in a small space

such as a mind or a bedroom. Memory is a much larger space of course

but these armies are not in there, they are in

here. Will you not help me at least with this, you

powers. The Pythian Goddess once sat here, fumes rising from her into the

early dawn. My person had fallen into a moment's rest so was sleeping

and missed her. So how do I know this? At any rate it is the bloody shiny

campaigns I need to watch—one by one, in greatest detail—

run through their course, over all

the continents, through every one of the centuries.

There was a time when there were no centuries.

It is what began with them my person needs to review.

There is not much time and it needs to do it all.

The sickness: new doctors come every day, I send them

away. I read the *Desk Reference.* I am on page 293.

You can see it open here, and all the underlining.

The disease is not as bad as the remedies. I try

them all. I will try them all till it is over.

How do I tell my person it is not my body that is ill.

Not my body, not me, that is right. To be sure, there *is*

terminal illness, but this is not personal, there is no longer

personal illness. No. It is something else.

Outside: seasons, what is left of them, a household, what is

said and done, ashes cleaned up again, a new fire set, bread, promises

called-out from one room to another, solid floors,

and then motion, motion all day long,

its miraculous invisible millions of paths

all over everything. *That* is *that* says my body. Then there's *this*—my telling

to you, the me in me, the multiplication of persons, out of control....

What will my body do when the book is all read.

It will have had them all, the possible illnesses.

It will ask for others. The unknown ones.

That their symptoms be listed and brought to it.

It trembles. It is trembling. It will look back on even this with a memory

of devastating joy.

DISENCHANTMENT

I shift my self. It's me I shout to the tree out the window

don't you know it's me, *a* me—I really don't care what we call it,

this personhood—a hood isn't a bad thing, a place to live, a self-blinding.

The book tells me I can't see you,

it's all frames and lenses and you, you who have been here

three centuries it is said according to the knowledge,

you are but a little flash, a cloud taking form in my neuron chamber, my

                                             brainpan,

in your *site* of my manufacturing of you—

not to mention all the cultural variables—that I am white, a woman, live in

x, earn my means via y—in a

city, on a portion of the globe where empire collects its secrets—where I

am one of its secrets—prey to the fine dust of its ideology,

which slips into my very gaze this dawn,

right there into the brainstem along with the feeding-in of

your more than seventy-two shifts in the nature of the vertical

just in your most upward-reaching ranking branch [I counted],

which will take, in about 6 minutes, the very first ray of sun coming over the

                                          rooftops—

branch which also took the full moon's laving down its left flank—

though only on about a fifth of the trunk last night

when I went out to measure it and looked up through the empty branches—

and Orion there above, and next to him others,

everything in its span of being—flesh, wood-fiber, star, moon, the matter

we keep finding names for in the invisible,

the matter we keep finding names for in the *far*—nowhere, nowhere does the circle

close, each thing has its own

expression, everything—if you stand very still—everything

manifesting its own version of fullness—tree, gaze,

muscle of my right hand gripping bark,

quiet which will be shattered by

backfire 3 minutes hence

in the passing car—striated petals of the as-yet-unseen crocus this soil over your root

now holds,

yellow not-yet-being-here of their yellow—but you,

are you truly invisible, unknowable, unreachable, specter of transience

only my own and not ever my own? So that I too am spectral now?

I can destroy you but I cannot know you?

When I come downstairs now and out to you,

to put my arms around you as far as is possible,

I come to the instant you have been growing towards for centuries

under this loud sky.

All day long over centuries even right now today—here—

*

"Instantly she was annoyed with herself for saying that. Who had said it? Not she; she had been trapped into saying something she did not mean. She looked up over her knitting and met it and it seemed to her like her own eyes meeting her own eyes, searching as she alone could search into her mind and her heart, purifying out of existence any lie. She praised herself in praising it, without vanity, for she was stern, she was searching. It was odd, she thought, how if one was alone, one leant to inanimate things; trees, streams, flowers; felt they expressed one; felt they became one; felt they knew one; in a sense were one; felt an irrational tenderness thus. She looked as for oneself. There rose—and she looked and looked with her needles suspended—there curled up off the floor of the mind, rising from the lake of one's being, a mist, a bride to meet her lover.

"What brought her to say that: 'we are in the hands of the Lord?' she wondered. The insincerity slipping in among the truths roused her, annoyed her. She returned to her knitting again."

You have to recover hope says the moon. Are you
kidding? I reply. The moon rises further. No,
you have to think about the whole situation from some *other*
perspective. Like how? My head is full of blood. So is
my mouth. The moon is full. Did you already know that
somehow, before I said it here, I ask. I need to know
what is inside your head. I don't know how to trust you.
This tree: could they take it away from me just by a way of
thinking? Will I ever know if I know it?
By any means? In this my one lifetime, here, on
this place? The high screams above, where the birds
seek landing, are there, the spots where the birds have, each, just been,
are there—glowing even though not in
the visible—others below fight over the road—
now *that* is a thing which exists, no one to quarrel over the fact of the road, no,
nor the night, which is cold and fine, in which nothing is deemed to be either
possible nor impossible. No, the centuries the ideas the engines circling,
the real ones with their sirens, and the ones of the mind, yes, giants are on their knees
but the mind is going along, fractioning, discerning, making categories by which to card
this from that this from that—ghosts of children at their game around their
tree—watch, they are disappearing as we summon them—now that
                                        is quite a trick,
wouldn't you say, this thing the mind can do—take it away as it gives it
                                        to you—
proving NOTHING exists—the particular deepness of understory shadow, for
example, which in deep summer, in childhood, slides over from shade to terror—
or watching wind make one branch strike the wall again and again—
or afternoon light darkening the side of the tree it does not strike,

and how that dark is filled with tenderness—why?—even a smell I could call "sweet"—
why?—as when the hawk lifts off the limb against his will because I've
stopped beneath to watch—(nailed to the sky the hawk is real, I have the right
to stay)(to see)—(why)—keep following this road my soul tells me and you'll find out—

                                                                                    yes—

stand in the disenchantment now and try to summon it, this thing the mind
is trying to give you—your freedom!—try to breathe-in its
absolutely clear air… amid the stubble, amid the shiny stones,
thinking *that part of my life is over.*

                                        *

Something has been sold to get here, something of mine, something perhaps
                                                    very precious
to me, an heirloom, an inheritance, I'm not sure what to call it.

                                        *

Oh radical mind—you who have come from afar and who must now live
among us—teach me from scratch how to love. Keep me kind.

PRAYING *(Attempt of Feb 6 '04)*

(For Emily)

I wake up in time, it is still dark.

Take the familiar position.

If I open my eyes I know what there will be: nothing.

No, really, nothing. So must keep them

shut, face in hands, hands holding eyes shut.

I search for gratitude, as if feeling around in a

park after nightfall for a lost hat,

gratitude, my closed eyes go everywhere.

It seems easy to do this but it's not.

Whom I stand-in for is not clear.

I operate on myself. The operation is never

successful. And you. Because it *is* an attempted

mouth-to-mouth. Henry watches from the wings

and cheers us on. But the manyness of our souls now

is not the manyness of his. The aim is to become

                         something broken

that cannot break further. Of course when one cries out

one makes everyone uncomfortable. Crooked, crooked.

That my loved ones exist. That they are right this

                     second still in

life. No one dying right now. Last person died

last month don't think about that. We are here. That

others I will never know are being killed in my name—by

us—oh what is that—that *us?* Gratitude for the trees

and the birds they house. The groundwater

not drinkable anymore—as of

last Spring. The modified corn having done that.

Hunger *in birds.* I try to hold that in mind, there is

no place for it.

Hunger in humans—there, I *can* do that.

No gratitude yet. Gratitude:

would acceptance

do. Inside my eyes

the blood vessels of my own *looking* which I

can see: a parched red desert, no rain for

centuries it would seem. I ask the doctor

if everyone

has this place

inside their eyes—these fields of

drought, deep fissures in sun-hardened clay. Yes,

he says, matter of factly. Matter-of-factly is the

gods' way

with us right now. We are in *consequence.*

The seeds are the ones *we* planted. "They"

can just sit back, watch it all grow. Jack's beanstalk for

example. The corn. Soon the soil which has it

in it

to bring forth

barley, wheat, rye, soy, alfalfa, hops, will no longer be good

for anything but hybrid corn. But each thing

is born as expected, even the corn plant,

so loud in my mind, thick greens, reticulated tassels—cell by cell

dividing to seize-up the tiniest strand of light and turn it into

the sinewy

visible. I love you I try to say from the floor.

To what? Somebody persuade me.

Words no longer prophesy. The third eye has an

infection or an allergy the doctor can't tell he gives it drops.

The feathers of the extinct, they are going to pile up where?

The possible feathers, the ones recalled by us for a while longer in great

detail—the geometry of the way the head

turned, the white stripe under the wing—where?

The cell-information of the bird just now in this hour in

this second going extinct, where is that information

going to be stored. I am afraid. "Everything must

exist in some form even extinction" I try. Like a breath

after the sentence is uttered, done, mouth shut with

meaning. That breath is in the air, isn't it, literally *in it*—

an exam of some kind would find them, the breath-molecules—no?—

and the *said thing?*—well, yes, it too is there, somewhere—

and the music—god what an orchestration—of all the footsteps

at once, right now, on this planet, I will not list all the surfaces

they tap against, I *will* put in all the grammars playing themselves out

in *all* the languages, spidery, all speaking at once, wind moving through

the corn, the speakers speaking stopping listening speaking.

I see the trunks of first-growth being piled. I try to imagine all the doorways

on the planet, bodies passing through, followed by light.

A name called out. An age [exact!] attached to

each body. And garments. And all the invisible fingers that move so rapidly

to make those garments. And factories, archipelagoes, more factories. This is

not going in a good direction. I think of all the hearts

beating right now—first in all the humans of all

the sizes, then add the animals,

the dying person with his strong young heart, the about-to-be

born with his heart eating up time. Starting to eat it. Hunger. Each beat

a clench of muscle. Worldwide orchestration of

                       so many darks

to hold so many clenchings. Also see

all the chests ripped open. Then no. Try to unsee.
Elders. Where are the real elders. They should be
at the head of the line here, all of us on our knees on the
floor should have guidance. But if I open my eyes I'll see
the hole that's in the dark, actually, and, you know,
you can go in barefoot all you like into there, holding water out in your
cupped hands, not a drop leaking, and time, your
time, is still being used up—tap tap, click click—I hear a cricket in the corn
start up. Summer leaps all over the tops of the full-grown plants,
all along the miles of fields. Then it's the blood. Blood
falling through all the dark enclosings of
bodies—animal, human, bird, reptile—blood. Doctor,
what proportion of this globe is water, what soil, what blood, what bone,
what breath exhaled, what (at any given moment) breath inhaled—how many
tons of air are inside bodies at *this* given
moment. Don't breathe. Hold it in. I won't
breathe. Here now. The dying mother in the waiting room with me
is talking with her daughter. She won't be here ever again soon. They have

                                               a brochure

spread out between them, a training program, involves some travel, can't

                                                             see really

what it is. This, says the young girl, pointing, this, mom,
this part here is the part I'm excited about.

PASSENGER

Where are you from. I have never been there. Why
did you leave. Excuse me. I cannot hear you. Because
of the partition. Is there some way you could lower
the partition. Where is your country. How many family
did you leave behind. Behind—is that what you would call
your country. Was it worth it. I can't imagine
what you have seen. Your desert your mountains your
endless blue rivers. *Blue rivers.* Your dirt cities. Your, your—oh what
is it, I have seen it in pictures, or things like it.
But *your* country. Your tiny piece of
country. Do you regret. I always ask you this. You keep on
changing there in the front seat driving me to my
destination. The destination changes. But the
movement is the same. You are making [not enough] money.
Not enough. You are on the phone, or your country's
radio is blasting. Over your new country your old country's radio.
Or you are stoned. Or you are very angry. Scores fly
through the small space between us. Someone *is* wrong.
That is one firm truth. But you see I cannot
do any right thing here any longer. I can think and
out-think and so on. But we're at the gates of
Judgment and you are still driving I am still the passenger.
We could change places. You see of course it's only on this page
we can do that. I will be the one who is
sleeping when I as a passenger arrive at the stand and knock at the front
window, or simply open the back door. *Wake up.* I will be the one
abruptly awakened. I will be sorry to awaken you. I will say you

didn't wake me I wasn't sleeping. I will say ok. You
will say I was just thinking. I will say of what. We are
now pulling away from the curb. I will say I was thinking of
my country. I count out my money again. I use this word *enough*.
We are approaching the destination. I am afraid.
I am afraid I will not be able to handle your suffering.
But that is a lie. You are so far away now from
your country—you have had to give up something so great
[God only knows what][I don't know what] for money,
I mean let's face it, for money to send home, yes, and then
to get all the stuff—not very much it is true but they make
you feel it is always almost *enough*. Also you are scared
[therefore the flags on your windows][one in the car itself].
Scared they will say you did IT. Or could have. I
am also scared. Am I driving now? It is not clear here.
There were supposed to be instructions. Stage directions.
Or signs from the deities, but they have moved on. There
must be an *other* place I think sometimes. For them to have
moved on to. The Apocalypse? That is a common
destination spot for many human minds now. The
rapid swallowing of all we made. The bird's-eye view we're
so in love with. Ah. Is this town empty? We keep on
driving. You, you who have come here abandoning what you
should not have abandoned (we both know this), what
cordless thing thundering with gold were you imagining when you boarded

> your bus
> away

fast, lake in the distance? The heroic wanderings of your

> own past people,

what have they come down to here, you glowingly immersed in cablight, in the jagged sums you take home to make

ends meet. In the humming exchange rates for what you send

home. Do you love them still? Here I see your eyes in the rear

view. Ah. How many names can you name. Of people who are

true Americans. The flags plastered on this vehicle block my view

everywhere. How many will cover for you. How many

of your names

have you changed. Have you attended to

your outfit.

Do you sing it well, the god-sanctioned anthem. Are you

fluent in *this* one-god's country. I know your country also has

one god but read the fine print he is not the

same as ours. "Ours." How does one peel this sticky

nationhood off. The vehicle keeps moving I can only be its

good passenger. You shut your eyes. You slumber and watch

the suburbs go

by. You tilt your glance to an aesthetic point of view. You shepherd

all the

interesting details. You "learn" how "others" live. Ah. End of the

Republic. How your outskirts flow by on this way away

from you. Your poor trapped immigrant driving your un-

imaginable sums around in his heart. Your balance sheet the road

to him. His balance sheet enough to make you fear if you

still fear. So long. Fearlessness of the American.

How you are hated. Everywhere. So long.

COMMUTE SENTENCE

of this prisoner, supreme commander, it is in your power—it says here in all
the books—of *all* the believers—it is within the scope of your authority. This
prisoner is innocent. This, the soul of the wee, is willing to collaborate,
                                        is willing to give up immediate
gratification. Do you know this. Is there a government out there? There are many
small things that are willing to do with the least water possible, the least power,
                                                                    the least
affection, the very least feeding—just enough will do—the minimum. The sentence
is incomprehensible to those of us almost-innocent who still have to see, for example,
this three fingers' width of gold-yellow crocus come up into the first light of
a February day—*which day* is not a right question, not now, not
with punishment incomprehensible laid upon us
exactly as the first rays of sun are [so indelibly] laid down on
our shoulders, our necks, the backs of our heads, as if a heavy
hand of blessing. Which says goodbye as it blesses.
You, you who were supposed to be just a *passage,*
everything seems to recognize you and bend your way.
Strangers in lobbies, in mosques. These tiniest thin-leaved drops
with their petals spinning, twisting—almost horribly—towards you that you
might open them. *Open them!* How deep did you want
to see in? Whatever is it we could be hiding inside
these hearts? Or, better yet—(because such a hat-trick
for you)—inside these minds. There should be a number
assigned so we know our turn. There should be an exact amount of
breaths we each get from Day One so we
know when. It took us much pain
to move from the river of retribution to the tree of

law. Why should that tree always become the killing tree?
There are many—not all—who would and *can*
utter the right syllables and their prayers should *convince.*
Not that there should be anyone to receive the prayer.
Not that there should be justice. No. We can be more alone
than that. History has worn us away and we are good now
at being on our hands and knees. The milk glass is filled with
lye. Megaphones scream goodmorning as if they were sunshine
and we were the new shoots. The Abyss has gone plural.
Flagpoles gleam and their stays click against them
in the thinning air. Time of the flags is long past—how
strange—a Flag! *Of what?* Are you a
nation, *you,* you there. Are you *in* a nation. Is one in you?
Are you at war or at peace or are war and peace
playing their little game over your dead body?
No, if you are like me. We will sit here. Will sit stubbornly
in this dock—which might look like a living
room or a bedroom—and stay put until, having taken
our prints our photographs our sleep our shynesses
our somethingness and our nothingness, having sanded us down
to dark things in dark, they will tell us what it is
we have done. I will not leave until I am charged
specifically. The brow of the whale is still in my
mind where I saw it go under, its last eye looking at
me *to return my stare.* When the water closed over,
you would never have known there had been anything
there.

COPY

(Attacks on the Cities, 2000–2003)

1.

How can I come across to you? What is it can be brought back, and from
where? Or no, that doesn't matter, forgive my question, I need not know *from
where*. Only that whatever rains down on us is meant to? Is just?
Oh Savior, pour upon me the Spirit, annihilate the Selfhood
in me, be Thou all my life. [Blake, "Jerusalem"]. From susansontag@
susansontag.com, re: amnesty international: the Nigerian Supreme Court has upheld
the death sentence for Amina Lawal, condemned for the crime of adultery August

19, 2002, to be

buried

up to her neck and stoned, her death postponed until now so that she
could continue nursing her baby, if you haven't been following the

case, Amina's baby

is regarded as evidence. Amina's case is being handled
by the Spanish branch of Amnesty. It will only take you a few seconds
to sign Amnesty's online petition. Please sign the petition now, copy this message
into a new email and send it to everyone in your address book. Dear Susan. Have

signed, have

copied and pasted, have sent. Dear Amnesty, have prayed, have nursed, have

copied,

have pushed send. Have nursed thoughts and pushed send. Have
sent again. Only my head is sticking out. My body is disappearing into

the soil.

Soul says *I would be saved.* God replies *And I would save.* Their dialogue
continues: "I would be pierced/And I would pierce/I

would be

[74]

born/And I would bear/I would be eaten/And I would eat.
Also I would be heard. Also am a Door to thee, who knockest
at me. [Also more here and there about the bonds
of love]. Also even this crumb of life I owe. To be struck by you.

2.

Where one must find ways to take cover. Where one must run
quickly as possible, hoping to catch the opening between
                              attacks. Across alley. Into
shelter. Must hide. Must hide under something, find silence. Find
where there is no one looking. Leave no prints.
Hope the moon is dark, far away as possible, far.
Far from where the earth trembles, mind trembles, buildings fall.
As if they were always waiting to return to earth.
Giddy the bodies in among all the possessions. The building-blocks of
                                        the normal
                                        full of flying
windows. The flowerpots crossing the fleeing
photographs. The birds. The finally emptying drawers. I saw
a shower of pens falling faster than the papers, slower than
the young girl. Books facing downward, wings-out.
Chairs on their backs in the downgoing.
Vases cradling their water midair.
One still gripping its silent bouquet.
Gloves, trays, uneaten sandwiches. The radio falling
transmitting the Mozart. The clock its seconds. The hat's long
                              zigzag, the one
high-heeled shoe. Headfirst some of the people, others not.
One who blindfolded himself,
one who is holding on to a coat. What is it

can rain further than this, what is there left that has not undergone its fall?

Something can die that is not alive. Something can open the air and show you

millions of roads. Is this not a richness then, that there be so many paths

of downwardness and all of them heretofore

invisible to us? Do not cry—do not cry out—for even if you cannot

                                        hear me, nor I

you, even if each path can be traversed but once, so it is a knowledge

that cannot be acquired, nor transmitted, nor used—even if it is a nothing

                              of a certain kind—even if

from where you are hiding now—no curl of smoke giving you away, millions of facts

there at your ready—from where you are, from where you are compelled

                                                    to be,

good and evil are the only alternatives.

3.

Morality

leads the soul to the frontiers of the Absolute and even

gives it an impulse to enter, but this

              is not enough. This

movement of Freedom cannot succeed unless there is

equivalent movement within the Absolute itself.

I am waiting. I am copying. *Equivalent movement within the*

Absolute.

4.

We have to remember that we are human. Something

                                  said

that. It is in me, that

[76]

something. But see how I now
     want
to place it *in you*. Human. As in having no privileged access to
knowledge of our own mind. Or of the world. Although we
think otherwise. To place it deep in you. That it *trouble*
you. You. Yes, it is true, someone is always crying out for you to listen.
Out from the screen. Where they play tricks with the soul.
Where they cry out "whosoever brings forth the bitterness most vividly,
whosoever makes us laugh when the blood shoots forth
from the open mouth of an other—any other—
from the open chest, cut throat, penetrated eye,
severed hand, arm, leg, cock, ear, severed artery wherever accessible—
what a thing the body, what a citadel, so penetratable—ah—
never never again to be tricked into believing
a thing so breakable could house a soul!—whosoever
makes us laugh at the scattered limbs, blades still flashing
from the hands of the killers, the giddy heat
on/off on/off in the eyes of the dead—yes—close-up on that—end of
shot, end of scene—whosoever makes us feel
we are among those left at the end—oh lucky few—how very special we are
in our seats, ticket in hand—*among*
the survivors—worth the price of admission—yes yes let that one, that maker of
          our virtual
selves, replacer of the heavy-headed virtuous self [or were you elsewhere
when it all went down] let him, let him get the prize." And see, they cheer,
even the candle on my table here seems hellbent to bend in the direction of
this wind. Even my best friend the grass seems to be whispering burn me.
I'll pay the price shouts the city. I wish to be lost gurgles spiritus mundi
folding over and over in the hot winds. And the heart interrupts itself.
And the heart interrupts itself again. Whizz. So dizzy. This could almost be

transcendence. Reader, listen to me. I know I am being cornered.

I hear the ironic tones I'm not dumb. I hate them as much as anyone they're such

a waste of time. To the question "Why is there something rather than

nothing," I still have no reply. I remember forget remember. I imagine I can posit

infinitude then it all collapses, poof, and there's just me and you, then of

course

just me, then nothing but the writing. This is a poem about wanting to survive.

It must clearly try anything.

5.

Something keeps you up at night, though.

Something must. What is it. What is it keeps you up at night.

Let no one persuade you you do not exist. Yes yes

you too are destined to die. But not before you have done something.

What will that be? Your death will not be *yours,* that is for sure. So:

whose will it be? Whose? Please.

And what are you situating in the future? And what are you making

present?

Listen: exclude yourself from the world, now, you can do

it, it is a practice. Say no to each part. Start with the right

hand, the left, the right eye, the left, *no* to the mouth. *No no* to the chest—keep

going—cut it all away, put yourself away, speech away, hope away, eliminate,

restore

nothing—take yourself out of the prison—out of the organic—you are not

breathing now—eyes closed go on I will keep speaking you can trust me—now,

is there a solution, look back at us, here, waiting, counting, the water running

out, the animals dying, the soil turning to dust, any wind too much wind,

dry, waste, the rulers in their controlled environments, the grasses gone at

the root, the birds in drifts at the feet of the trees—see—nothing at all—
the mother is being killed and you are watching but really, as with all of us,
even this witnessing is tiring. Look away. Look away, poor thing.

6.

[In my dream the God said we have to change everything
again. *Again?* I said. *Why?* Because, it said. Because.]

7.

[Then it said Pause Pause Pause Pause.]

PRAYING *(Attempt of April 19 '04)*

If I could shout but I must not shout.

The girl standing in my doorway yesterday weeping.

In her right hand an updated report on global warming.

An intelligent girl, with broad eyes and a strong

wide back. What am I supposed to tell her?

Outside the trees seem healthy to me, and the street is filled

with human busyness. Oh street. Built to conduct

all of our errands and appointments and even some secret running to

assignation. I feel now all the streets holding us up

as if they had a kind of patient willingness—no hopelessness—

just holding till it is time to be opened and undone.

The map of my city plays itself over my eyes, a piece

of vibrant lacework—of which I have seen the first

11th-century sample—which took the eyesight of the 12-year-old

assigned it. Lace where the knots of the individual

strands

are too small for the human eye as we know it to see.

Has the human eye changed. The eye doctor asks me

if it is more like dust or soil, the matter my eye splays

against the empty walls. More like dust. Then it's ok.

It's really my own blood I see.

It will disintegrate, just not right away. When it goes

from dust to soil I should come back. Writing this

has been a very long detour I know.

No one likes to lie or be lied to.

Do I ask the help of the four walls and the hard

soil-covering street

to answer the student still standing here?
The answers are unknown, but the possible truths
forbidden. Because we cannot ask another to live
without hope. Above—above all this—I have lived out my
life. Indulgent with hope. Given freedom to wonder.
To mull, speculate, praise.
Oh Lord what do I do with the great desire to praise.
The frenzied joy of detail. The fullness of
existence I feel in *contradiction.* I confess I love the
surface. The surface of all creation. Its absence of
feeling. Its presence of *sensation.* How do I stay awake
for this. The slumber is upon me. How I said to the girl
it would be all right *in the end.* Not to worry. There

                                            was

another suicide here last week. One must be so careful
re the disappearance of hope. A new illusion must present
itself immediately. When I pray now
this is what I pray for. That the girl not stand like this
in the doorway, with her facts on the sheet in her right hand,
hardly able to find a normal breath. The verdict
is irreversible. Meaning the word cannot be taken back.
It is said. It is said. That is what the boy who jumped

                                  left in his note.

Knocking against a stone wall says the poet
knowing the wall will not yield to any im-
ploration. But the poet lived when there was a wall
[take away wall]. The poet lived when imploration
rose up in the human throat. When hands rose to
knock. The girl in my doorway, more terrified
by the lack of terror in the *others*—"where are all the

others" she is crying, "why does no one know, why

is this *not being reported*"—how is she supposed to bear

the silence. Someone must implore.

Someone must expect yield.

She wants the desire to cry out.

She does not want us to

go down singing. I might. She doesn't. She can be

soothed today, friend, but not tomorrow. Tomorrow she

will jump out a window or pick up a gun or believe

with a belief that hums so loudly no human reason

will ever reach into that hive again, that whatever

happens

will be ordained. All will be a sign.

You will never again be able to scare her.

A story so firm it will abolish the future.

Coming in to grip the thing we call Time.

Don't tell her she's wrong when she comes to your

doorsill.

Let her weep. Do not comfort. Do not give false

hope.

Tell her to tell the others. Let the dream of contagion

set loose its virus. Don't let her turn away.

I, here, today, am letting her cry out the figures, the scenarios,

am letting her wave her downloaded pages

into this normal office-air between us. 19 April. 2004.

I do not know what to tell her, Lord. I do not

want her

to serve you. Not you. Not you above all.

COMMUNION

Come here. Open your eyes. Open your mouth.

The years that enter us are also visitors.

For the host we must make extra accommodations.

As in open your mouth. Become an actor. Act.

Some approach on their knees, how slow, do they not want

to leap. Leap! There's no such thing as time I

think—not knowing at all if that is true.

Lie down. Stand up. Open your mouth.

Awaiting you is a thing like a knot.

You bite down hard, it takes you up.

Not unlike in the circus, yes, you are an

                            acrobat.

If there is an orchestra, sometimes there is,

everyone is playing at different speeds.

Imagine that sound. Now imagine

                    this act of

obedience, then open your mouth [that

                        sound]

[which we cannot hear][but which another order

                          might] then

take in the cacophony,

the multifariousness, no one hearing his neighbor.

Bite down, swallow.

There, there is the tone.

Everyone can hear it.

The rough note works. Trust it.

An anchor drops and waves swing over it. Sinks.

Right through the forwardgoing swell.

Finds bedrock. Catches. Above

strong easterlies fuss all the waves towards shore.

The swell gets bigger, smaller. Down, down the anti-

                                      buoyant

anchor, spreading its eye of opening water—a moment, a

                                 gaze—then the

shutting over. The ear opens as well. Because what we

                              are listening for

is believed to be audible

over great distances.

We wait—we have been waiting—for reputable observers.

Are we to become those observers ourselves?

How far will it travel. Where exactly is

sound lost? It is a shape. Then it begins to

                        no longer be

a shape. Clacks as little piles of stones

collapse. Birds then insect-stitch. Vacancy and then, in it,

the sound of a plough? The sound of flight—wind, wing?

Infection? Description? Open up says

the god but we fear contagion. Shouldn't we

bite down and be the sacrifice we long to be but do we

                           really?

Are you a statistical error? Is it the moon or

a destination spot that is almost *full?*

Try, friend, try to live in the solar system now

instead of "the world." Look up: the moon

is to be *occupied:* now look at the

tree in the field. Why does it feel

the moral questions are all-bets-off when

the new real estate on Mars

beams back and trading begins?

Your neighbor at dinner mentions it.

You think at first what is this meal, right here,

in front of me. The moon glides by out the

dining room window and you shudder with nothing

resembling sorrow as the

next course arrives.

POSTERITY

I have talked too much. Have hurried. Have tried to cover the fear
with curiosity. Also amazement. It is fear. Also know that a poem
is, in the end, not supposed to scare you, sweet friend, reader,
I believe you to be a person who would hide me if it came to that.
Wouldn't you? Whoever I am or happen to be.
Who would remove the wood planks in the floor, in the
ceiling, let me in to enough breathing space. A person who
will not walk by the man old enough to be your grandfather,
somebody's grandfather, on the street, in this great cold.
What is the question? What is the current nature of the Grail?
The Grail: "consistently identified with the relics of Christ's
blood or with the vessel used by Him at the last
supper. Or with both. The cult of Holy Blood."
Let us now turn to this, as the instructor says. We
turn. To somebody's person, on the street, in this great cold.
The earliest record of the Holy Blood comes from
Mantua—804. This is reliably reported
but seems to have been lost again.
Know I am supposed to use the poem, however sorry,
to lift the subject to a place of beauty. The very term: "beauty": do you
                                        hear that? Old man
unable to even ask for anything anymore. The one without a written plea on
                                        piece of card-
board. The one just standing there by the door of the 7/11 so
drunk or stoned or hungover and *cold* he cannot even remember
                                        he is supposed
to ask—that is his role here in this hall of mirrors—ah friend—that man,

do you know him, the one I have to suppose you *will not walk past,* although what
you will do after that is anyone's guess.
I put my hands in my pockets. I fish out change.
Sometimes bills if I can. Of course I am confused. I do not know
                                    the right thing to do.
Last week leaving with a newspaper and some juice I gave him
the juice. In November, when we had bought a ready-cooked chicken
for our dinner I handed him the chicken. It was in a paper bag with aluminum
lining. Even so it was extremely hot. I gave it him in both hands.

                                    I hadn't
                                    realized it
was too hot for hands that are too cold. The aluminum also.
You should know the aluminum only protects from burning
those hands living life at *room temperature.*
This was explained to me later after he burned his hand, but first
he couldn't hold it so I told him to sit down, helped him
down. Found a way to place the chicken beside him went back in
to the convenience store. Got paper towels. Came back.
Him just staring at it. It long past a thing he could
register. Went back in. Got a plastic knife and fork. Got more paper and a paper
                                    plate. Had to
                                    buy these.

Thought it would have been better to give him the cash.
Then thought, no, that just goes to liquor. Where are we?
You who have helped me, Buber, Kafka, Dr. Robinson—you, hunger specialists,
where are we? I am sitting beside him saying Sir this is for you
to *eat* [it is loud on JFK Street, also Thanksgiving traffic].
I rip open the package and realize we are too
exposed, move him further into the doorway, say
Sir, this is some dinner for you, Sir—he is just looking

out—may I help you, ripping the bag then feeling for

the bones, a piece ripped off, a piece on the plate, a knife,

a fork. I see I must take his hand. I take his right hand. It is full of bones,

very little flesh. I pull his jacket round.

I put the chicken near. He looks at the piece then the

bag. It will get cold Sir, it would be good to eat

while hot. Grief walks by us.

I have to leave. Of course I have to leave. As always am

expected. As always have done nothing. What, what is it

that is

so near death it is willing to take

any love it can get? Wrote a poem with the lines

"how can I write/in a lyric poem that the world we live in/

has already been destroyed? It is true. But/it cannot be said

into the eyes of an other,/as that other will have nowhere

to turn." Took the lines out. Thought "what should be the *subject*."

Forgive me I am perhaps not speaking to you individually.

You are perhaps among the exceptions [actually I'm not sure there are

exceptions][make of the grief a kind of beauty that might

endure].

Oh I have talked too much.

To praise to recall to memorialize to summon to mind

the thing itself—forgive me—*the given thing*—that you might have persuaded yourself is

invisible,

unknowable, creature of context—it is there, it is there, it needs to be there. I awaken

again. The

man, last night, his hands

no longer operational.

I wake up operational

over what country now.

The rain has ceased,

I stare at the gleaming garden.

NOTES

Overlord: in November 1943 Stalin, Churchill, and Roosevelt met in Tehran and agreed the Allies would mount a major offensive, opening a second front, in Europe. General Eisenhower was put in charge of what became known as "Operation Overlord," which included the landing on Omaha Beach, in the Normandy region of France, on what came to be known as D-Day: June 6, 1944. It is customary for the military to denote days prior to, and after, that day with a plus or minus sign, as well as designating the scheduled hour of the invasion as H Hour.

"Praying (Attempt of June 6 '03)": the quotes from Simone Weil are from *Waiting for God*, translated by Emma Craufurd, introduced by Leslie Fiedler.

"Praying (Attempt of June 8 '03)" refers to the confusion inflicted by storm and riptide upon the Allied landing plan in the first hours of June 6. The beach known as Omaha, which lies below the towns of Vierville, Les Moulins, Saint Laurent, and Colleville, had been divided by the planners of the landing into sectors known as—starting furthest west, at Vierville—Charlie, Dog Green, Dog White, Dog Red, Easy Green, Easy Red, Fox Green, and Fox Red. These beaches were more heavily fortified than had been imagined, and the men came under heavy fire from bunkers on the cliffs above them. In general, the most disastrous pileups of landing craft off course occurred at Dog Green (under Vierville) and Dog Red/Easy Green (under Saint Laurent). At Dog Green, for example, the 116th, Company A, lost almost all its officers in the first fifteen minutes. Members of G Company were dragged off target to Dog White and Dog Red. Although at first more protected by smoke upon landing, they were confounded, having landed in areas not assigned to them, and unable to understand landmarks. The second wave of soldiers found themselves landing in a tide rising rapidly towards the shore's seawall, and in waters filled with many of the wounded and dead. The three lines in quotation are from Keith Douglas's *The Complete Poems* (Faber and Faber). Douglas landed on D-Day and was killed on June 9, 1944.

"Soldatenfriedhof" is a literal account. My thanks to Lucien Tisserand, Conservateur of the German Military Cemetery at La Cambe. I am much indebted, as well, to the spirit of *Les Jardins de la Memoire*, by Annick Helias (with Françoise Avril, Dominique Bassiere, Paul Colin, and Patrick Galineau), for leading me to an on-site study of the military graveyards in Normandy.

"Spoken from the Hedgerows"(1): voices here are accurately named, and their trajectories towards the staging grounds for Operation Overlord in Britain are also accurate, although condensed, as recounted in *Voices of D-Day*, edited by Ronald J. Drez (Louisiana State University Press, 1994). By May 1944, almost 1,500,000 fighting men were bivouacked in Great Britain while awaiting action.

"Spoken from the Hedgerows"(2): the poem reimagines the voyages of the American D-Day glider attacks, and uses as its source *Glidermen of Neptune*, by Charles J. Masters (Southern Illinois University Press), as well as *D-Day Gliders, Les Planeurs Americains du Jour J*, by Philippe Esvelin, translated by John Lee (Edition Heimdal). The time frame envisioned here spreads from that of Missions *Detroit* and *Chicago* (scheduled before H Hour) to that of *Keokuk*, which was scheduled to fly over the invasion's naval forces, in daylight. *Detroit*'s landing time of 4:04 AM puts it at 146 minutes from the actual H Hour of 6:30 AM. *Keokuk*'s departure time of 18:30 puts it 12 hours after the first beach landings. Only Mission *Keokuk* used the "horsa" gliders alone. Missions *Detroit* and *Chicago* used "wacos," and the other missions of June 6 and 7 (*Elmira, Galveston,* and *Hackensack*) used both. The second section selects from FDR's much longer Radio Prayer Broadcast on D-Day, "Let Our Hearts Be Stout," printed in a special Tyophile broadcast edition.

"Spoken from the Hedgerows"(3) relies in part on *Parachute Infantry: An American Paratrooper's Memoir of D-Day and the Fall of the Third Reich* (Louisiana State University Press) by David Kenyon Webster, as well as on Stephen E. Ambrose's introduction to that book. "Fussell" refers to Paul Fussell, a junior officer in a rifle company during the war, and remarks in his book *Wartime*. The quotation is edited from a much longer piece. The quotations from Webster are from two letters—one to his parents after his first jump into Normandy, when he returned to England to prepare for his next jump, and a subsequent one to his mother alone. Kurt Gabel's remarks are from *The Making of a Paratrooper* (Lawrence, Kansas, 1990).

"Disenchantment" [p.43]: some language is used from Michael Kimmelman's "The Enigma: An Artist Beyond Isms," which appeared in the *New York Times Magazine* (January 27, 2002). Quotations from Goethe's *Faust* are from the Walter Kaufmann translation. This poem was commissioned by the San Francisco Art Museum for a special-edition book on the painter, *Richter 858*.

"Physician": this poem is for Rose and Bill.

"Disenchantment" [p.61] is for Bonnie Costello. The second section is quoted from Virginia Woolf's *To the Lighthouse*. It thinks back, as well, to Eric Auerbach's *Mimesis*.

"Copy": the quotation from Hafiz is from *Hafiz of Shiraz, Thirty Poems, Introduction to the Sufi Master*, translated by Peter Avery and John Heath-Stubbs (Handsel Books). The other quotations are noted, except one phrase in section 4 from *Philosophy in the Flesh*, by George Lakoff and Mark Johnson (Basic Books). Amina Lawal's sentence was overturned.

"Posterity": the words in italics beginning *"so near death"* are from the poem "To a Blossoming Pear Tree," by James Wright. This poem is dedicated to his memory and his work.

"Praying (Attempt of May 9, '03)": a different version of this poem first appeared under the title "Third" in the book *Bits & Pieces Put Together to Present a Semblance of a Whole* on the permanent collection of the Walker Art Museum. In an early re-working, the poem became a meditation on Barnett Newman's painting *The Third* (1962).

© PETER SACKS

ABOUT THE AUTHOR

Jorie Graham is the author of ten collections of poetry, including *The Dream of the Unified Field*, which won the Pulitzer Prize. She divides her time between western France and Cambridge, Massachusetts, where she teaches at Harvard University.